Unleashing the Power Within

The Journey to Personal Transformation

By: Raymond Penny

Printed in the United States of America.

ISBN: 979-8-858-40412-5

D E D I C A T I O N

In Loving Memory of my mom, Lyris Penny

Though I never had the opportunity to know you in person, your memory has always lived within my heart. This book is dedicated to you, a remarkable woman whose presence graced the world, even if only for a short while.

Through the stories and memories shared by loved ones, I have come to understand the depth of your love and the impact you had on those around you. Your kindness, strength, and unwavering spirit continue to inspire me each day.

While I may never experience your physical embrace or hear your voice firsthand, your spirit lingers, guiding me through life's ups and downs. Your gentle presence has become a warm and comforting force, reminding me of the endless love that flows between us.

This dedication serves as a tribute to your memory, a celebration of the beautiful soul that you were. Your absence has taught me the preciousness of every moment, and the importance of cherishing our loved ones while we have the chance.

I carry your legacy with me, Mom, woven into the fabric of my being. With every word I write, every step I take, and every achievement I reach, it is your unwavering belief in me that propels me forward.

Though my heart aches for the moments we cannot share, I find solace in knowing that you are watching over me from beyond the veil. Your love transcends time and space, connecting us eternally.

In dedicating this book to you, I honor the profound impact you have had on my life, even in your absence. Thank you for shaping me into the person I am today and for teaching me the enduring power of love.

Forever in my thoughts and heart,

Raymond M Penny

P R O L O G U E

A Glimpse into the Unknown

In the vast expanse of the universe, our individual lives are but fleeting moments in time. Yet, within each of these moments lies a unique and extraordinary story waiting to be told. It is here, within the depths of the prologue, that we shall catch a glimpse of the beauty and mystery that awaits us.

As we enter this realm of exploration, let us leave behind the shackles of familiarity and step into the realm of the unknown. It is a place where possibilities abound, where dreams can take flight, and where we can unearth hidden truths about ourselves and the world we inhabit.

With open hearts and minds, we embark on this journey together, embracing the uncertainty and embracing the mysteries that lie ahead. For it is through the act of stepping beyond our comfort zones that we discover the true essence of who we are and what we are capable of.

In the prologue, we will encounter fragments of wisdom, whispers of truth, and echoes of forgotten dreams. It is a space for reflection and introspection, where we can pause to contemplate the meaning behind our existence and the intricacies of our connections with others.

As your dedicated mentor and guide, I am here to

accompany you on this path, offering support, encouragement, and insight along the way. Together, we will navigate the uncharted waters of personal growth, delve into the complexities of human emotions, and marvel at the wonders that unfold before us.

But let us remember that this is not simply a solitary journey; it is one that we undertake together. Within the pages that follow, we will be joined by the stories and experiences of countless individuals who have traversed similar paths. Their narratives will serve as beacons of light, guiding us toward self-discovery, empathy, and understanding.

Through the chapters that lay ahead, we will explore the various aspects of our lives – relationships, personal development, resilience, and more. We will delve into the depths of our fears, celebrate the triumphs of our joys, and marvel at the resilience of the human spirit.

As we move forward, let us embrace the unknown with courage, curiosity, and a willingness to be transformed. The journey may be filled with twists and turns, but together we will navigate them with grace and acceptance.

In closing, dear reader, I invite you to take a deep breath and step into the prologue of this shared adventure. Let us embark on this transformative voyage, embracing the unknown, and opening ourselves up to the profound possibilities that lie within.

With boundless enthusiasm and anticipation.

C ONTENTS

F O R E W O R D

When embarking upon this literary journey, my heart is filled with a mixture of excitement and gratitude. It is an honor to have the opportunity to share these words with you, dear reader. Before we delve into the chapters ahead, I would like to take a moment to express my deepest appreciation for your presence within these pages.

This book is not just a collection of words, but rather a heartfelt invitation to embark on a shared experience. Through the turning of each page, we will discover the power of emotions, the beauty of human connections, and the triumphs that grace our lives. It is my hope that this exploration will inspire, comfort, and uplift you, reminding you of the boundless potential that lies within us all.

As I reflect upon the genesis of this project, I am reminded of the cherished memories and the profound impact of a remarkable individual who played an irreplaceable role in shaping who I am today - my mom, Lyris Penny. Her absence has left an indelible mark on my soul, one that has motivated me to explore the depths of human experiences through words and stories.

While this book may be mine to pen, it is a tribute to the countless individuals who have crossed my path, offering their love, support, and wisdom. Each encounter has contributed to the fabric of this narrative, illustrating the intricate tapestry of life.

Within these pages, we will delve into the profound emotions that make us human – love, joy, sadness, fear – and examine how they shape our perceptions, decisions, and relationships. We will explore the power of vulnerability, the courage to embrace change, and the transformative nature of forgiveness. It is my hope that, together, we can navigate these universal themes and find solace in the shared human experience.

Throughout this journey, I encourage you to reflect on your own story, for it is within the tapestry of your life that these words will find their true meaning. Let us embark on this adventure together, dear reader, as we discover the extraordinary within the ordinary and the beauty that lies in embracing the imperfect symphony of existence.

In closing, I extend my deepest gratitude to you, cherished reader, for accompanying me on this voyage. May these words serve as a gentle reminder of the interconnectedness of our shared human experience, and may they leave an indelible imprint upon your heart.

With love and gratitude,

INTRODUCTION

Welcome to "Unleashing the Power Within: The Journey to Personal Transformation."

This book is a guide to help you embark on a transformative journey toward unlocking your true potential and living a fulfilling life. In these pages, you will find wisdom, practical strategies, and guidance that will empower you to create positive change in every aspect of your life. In today's fast-paced and demanding world, it's easy to lose sight of our own dreams and aspirations.

We often find ourselves trapped in limiting beliefs, self-doubt, and fear, which hinder our personal growth and happiness. However, deep within each of us lies an extraordinary power to overcome these obstacles and thrive. The purpose of this book is to help you tap into that power by providing you with the tools, insights, and inspiration necessary for personal transformation. Whether you are seeking to improve your relationships, career, health, or overall well-being, this book will guide you toward unleashing your full potential.

Throughout the chapters, you will learn how to cultivate self-awareness, develop a growth mindset, and overcome self-limiting beliefs. You will discover powerful techniques to enhance your emotional intelligence, strengthen your resilience, and boost your confidence. Additionally, you will explore effective strategies for setting goals, creating positive habits, and managing your time effectively. It is important to note that personal transformation is not an overnight process. It requires patience, dedication, and a willingness to step outside of your comfort zone.

This book aims to support you through this journey, providing you with the guidance and encouragement you need along the way. By embracing the content within these pages, you will gain the tools necessary to break free from negative patterns, unlock your true potential, and live a life that aligns with your deepest values and desires. Ultimately, this book is not just about making changes, but about becoming the best version of yourself and living a life that brings you joy and fulfillment. So, are you ready to embark on this transformative journey?

Are you ready to unleash the power within you and create the life you've always envisioned? If so, let the adventure begin. Together, we will navigate the challenges, celebrate the victories, and unlock the extraordinary potential that resides within you. Get ready to embrace personal transformation and experience the profound impact it can have on your life. Let's start this empowering journey together, step by step, towards unleashing the power within you.

CHAPTER 1

THE CALL FOR CHANGE: RECOGNIZING THE NEED FOR PERSONAL TRANSFORMATION

In the vast landscape of our lives, there comes a moment when a whisper from within beckons us to embark on a journey of personal transformation. This call for change may manifest as a subtle feeling of restlessness, a yearning for something more, or a realization that our current way of living no longer serves our highest good. It is during these moments that we must pay attention and heed the call.

Recognizing the need for personal transformation is the first step toward embracing a life of growth, fulfillment, and purpose. It is an invitation to delve into the depths of our being, unearth our true desires, and unlock the dormant potential that lies within us. It is an acknowledgment that we are capable of more and that we have the power to create positive change in our lives.

However, it is important to note that this call for change may be met with resistance. Fear, uncertainty, and self-doubt often accompany the realization that we need to transform. We may question our ability to change, worry about leaving our comfort zones, or fear the unknown that lies ahead. Yet, it is precisely within these challenges that the greatest opportunities for growth arise.

In order to recognize the need for personal transformation, we must first become aware of the signs and signals that present themselves to us. These signs may appear in various forms - a dissatisfaction with our current circumstances, a sense of unfulfillment, or a longing for a deeper connection with ourselves and others.

They may also surface as repeated patterns of behavior that no longer serve us or as physical and emotional symptoms indicating that something within us is yearning to be addressed.

Once we become attuned to these signs, we must summon the courage to confront them head-on. This requires an honest examination of our lives, a willingness to acknowledge our shortcomings, and a dedication to embracing change.

It is a process of self-reflection and introspection, as we explore the thoughts, beliefs, and behaviors that have shaped our existence thus far.

Moreover, recognizing the need for personal transformation entails accepting that growth is a natural part of the human experience. It means acknowledging that change is not only necessary but also inevitable if we are to live authentic, purposeful lives.

By embracing this truth, we empower ourselves to step

into our full potential and create a future that aligns with our deepest desires. In conclusion, recognizing the need for personal transformation is the catalyst that ignites the fire within us.

It is the pivotal moment when we answer the call to embark on a journey of growth, self-discovery, and empowerment. By acknowledging this need and embracing change, we set ourselves on a path toward a more fulfilling life, where the possibilities for personal development are limitless.

So, let us heed the call, listen to the whispers of our souls, and begin our transformative journey with open hearts and open minds.

C H A P T E R 2

O V E R C O M I N G L I M I T I N G B E L I E F S : B R E A K I N G F R E E F R O M S E L F - L I M I T I N G P A T T E R N S

Within the depths of our subconscious minds, reside a series of beliefs that shape our perception of ourselves and the world around us. These beliefs, often ingrained from an early age, have the power to either propel us toward greatness or hold us back from reaching our full potential. They are known as limiting beliefs - negative thoughts or assumptions about ourselves and our abilities that sabotage our success and hinder personal growth.

To truly transform and embrace personal change, it is essential to identify and overcome these self-limiting patterns. We must become aware of the beliefs that imprison us, challenge their validity, and replace them with empowering beliefs that uplift and empower us.

Overcoming limiting beliefs requires a willingness to explore the depths of our psyche and confront the fears and insecurities that underlie these patterns. It is a journey of self-discovery, as we uncover the root causes of our self-doubt and negative self-talk. By understanding the origin of these beliefs, whether rooted in childhood experiences, societal conditioning, or past failures, we can begin to dismantle their hold on us.

One of the first steps in overcoming limiting beliefs is to challenge their accuracy and examine the evidence that supports them. Often, these beliefs are based on distorted perceptions or limited experiences. By questioning the validity of our assumptions and seeking alternative perspectives, we can gain a more balanced and realistic view of ourselves and our capabilities.

Furthermore, it is crucial to surround ourselves with a supportive and nurturing environment that encourages personal growth and positive self-belief. The influence of others plays a significant role in shaping our beliefs about ourselves.

By seeking out individuals who inspire and uplift us, we are more likely to adopt empowering beliefs and let go of the limitations imposed by others.

Overcoming limiting beliefs also requires a commitment to self-compassion and self-acceptance. It is important to realize that everyone has areas of self-doubt and areas for improvement. Embracing our imperfections and treating ourselves with kindness and understanding allows us to break free from the vicious cycle of self-sabotage and move toward personal growth.

In addition to self-compassion, cultivating a practice of positive affirmations and visualization can be powerful tools for overcoming limiting beliefs. By consciously reprogramming our minds with empowering statements and visualizing ourselves living our desired reality, we create new neural pathways that support our growth and transformation.

In conclusion, breaking free from self-limiting patterns and overcoming limiting beliefs is a crucial step in the journey of personal transformation. By identifying and challenging these beliefs, surrounding ourselves with a supportive community, practicing self-compassion, and engaging in empowering techniques like positive affirmations and visualization, we can release the constraints that hold us back and step into our true potential. Let us embrace the power within us to transcend our limitations and create a future filled with possibility and fulfillment.

CHAPTER 3

DISCOVERING YOUR TRUE SELF UNVEILING AUTHENTICITY

In a world that often encourages conformity, embracing our true selves and living authentically is a courageous act. It requires the willingness to peel back the layers of societal expectations, social conditioning, and our own masks to reveal the essence of who we truly are. This journey of self-discovery is a profound endeavor that brings forth a sense of freedom, fulfillment, and genuine connection with others.

To uncover our true selves, we must first cultivate self-awareness - an honest and non-judgmental observation of our thoughts, emotions, values, and desires. This self-reflection allows us to identify the authentic aspects of ourselves that may have been suppressed or hidden beneath layers of societal norms or personal insecurities.

Discovering our true selves also entails letting go of the need for external validation. Society often places emphasis on external factors such as appearance, achievements, and status, which can lead us to lose touch with our internal compass. By shifting our focus inward and seeking validation from within, we can tap into our unique gifts, passions, and purpose.

Unveiling authenticity requires embracing vulnerability

and embracing all facets of our being. It means showing up fully, flaws and all, and accepting ourselves unconditionally. Authenticity is not about being perfect or conforming to a particular image; it is about being real and genuine in every moment.

Furthermore, discovering our true selves involves aligning with our core values and beliefs. When we live in accordance with our values, we experience a sense of integrity and congruence that resonates deeply within us. By clarifying our values and making choices that reflect them, we can live a life that is true to who we are at the deepest level.

In addition to self-awareness and values alignment, it is essential to cultivate self-acceptance and self-love on this journey of authenticity. Embracing our strengths, weaknesses, and imperfections with kindness and compassion allows us to fully embrace our unique selves without judgment. By practicing self-care and nurturing our physical, mental, and emotional well-being, we create a solid foundation for self-discovery and genuine self-expression.

Finally, unveiling authenticity is a continuous process of self-exploration and growth. As we evolve and experience new insights, our true selves may continue to unfold and expand. It is a lifelong journey that requires patience, self-reflection, and a willingness to embrace the unknown.

In conclusion, discovering our true selves and living authentically is a transformative and liberating endeavor.

By cultivating self-awareness, letting go of external validation, embracing vulnerability, aligning with our values, and practicing self-acceptance, we can peel back the layers of societal conditioning and reveal the essence of who we truly are.

Let us embark on this journey of self-discovery with curiosity and courage, embracing our authentic selves and creating a life filled with purpose, connection, and fulfillment.

CHAPTER 4

SELF-AWARENESS: THE FOUNDATION OF PERSONAL GROWTH

Self-awareness is the cornerstone of personal growth, providing us with the necessary insights and understanding to navigate our inner world and make positive changes in our lives. It involves developing a deep understanding of our thoughts, emotions, behaviors, and patterns, allowing us to recognize our strengths, limitations, and areas for growth.

Self-awareness begins with a willingness to observe ourselves objectively, without judgment or criticism. It requires a gentle curiosity and a genuine desire to understand who we are at our core. By cultivating this mindset, we can uncover unconscious beliefs, biases, and conditioning that may be influencing our actions and decisions.

One way to enhance self-awareness is through self-reflection. Taking the time to pause, introspect, and ask ourselves meaningful questions allows us to delve deeper into our inner landscape. Through journaling, meditation, or simply sitting in quiet contemplation, we can gain valuable insights into our thoughts, emotions, and motivations.

In addition to self-reflection, seeking feedback from

trusted individuals can provide valuable perspectives on our blind spots and areas for improvement. It takes courage to receive constructive criticism, but by approaching it with an open mind and a willingness to learn, we can gain valuable insights that propel our personal growth.

Self-awareness also involves paying attention to our physical sensations and bodily cues. Our bodies often provide valuable information about our emotional state, stress levels, and overall well-being. By practicing mindfulness and tuning into our body's signals, we can develop a deeper understanding of ourselves and make choices that support our overall health and happiness.

Furthermore, self-awareness extends beyond just understanding ourselves; it also includes recognizing how we impact and interact with others. Developing empathy and emotional intelligence allows us to be more attuned to the needs and feelings of those around us. This understanding fosters healthier relationships and a greater sense of connection with others.

As we deepen our self-awareness, we gain clarity on our values, passions, and purpose. We become more aligned with our authentic selves and can make choices that are in harmony with who we truly are. This self-knowledge becomes the guiding force behind our personal growth journey, empowering us to make intentional decisions and pursue the path that resonates with our deepest desires.

In conclusion, self-awareness serves as the foundation of personal growth. By cultivating a non-judgmental mindset, engaging in self-reflection, seeking feedback, tuning into our physical sensations, and developing empathy, we can gain a deeper understanding of ourselves and our impact on others. This self-awareness allows us to make conscious choices, align with our values, and embark on a journey of personal growth and transformation. Let us embrace self-awareness as a powerful tool for self-discovery and create a life filled with authenticity, fulfillment, and continual growth.

CHAPTER 5

EMOTIONAL INTELLIGENCE: NURTURING EMOTIONAL WELL-BEING

Emotional intelligence, often referred to as EQ, is a fundamental aspect of our overall well-being and personal growth. It encompasses our ability to recognize, understand, and manage our own emotions, as well as empathize with and relate to the emotions of others.

By developing emotional intelligence, we can cultivate healthier relationships, make more informed decisions, and enhance our overall quality of life. Emotional intelligence begins with self-awareness, as discussed in the previous chapter.

By understanding and accepting our own emotions, we can better navigate through life's challenges and respond to others with empathy and compassion. This means identifying and acknowledging our feelings, whether they are positive or negative, and learning how to express them in a healthy and effective manner. Once we have developed self-awareness, we can then work on improving our emotional regulation.

This involves managing our emotions in a way that allows us to navigate difficult situations without being overwhelmed or reactive.

By practicing self-regulation techniques such as deep breathing, mindfulness, and reframing negative thoughts, we can maintain a sense of calm and make rational decisions even in the face of adversity. Another crucial component of emotional intelligence is developing empathy. Empathy is the ability to understand and share the feelings of others.

By actively listening and putting ourselves in someone else's shoes, we can better connect with their experiences and offer support and understanding.

This fosters stronger relationships, builds trust, and promotes a sense of belonging and community. Furthermore, emotional intelligence involves effective communication skills. This includes both verbal and non-verbal communication, as well as active listening.

By being aware of our own body language, tone of voice, and choice of words, we can ensure that our messages are clear, respectful, and considerate. Additionally, by listening attentively and seeking to understand rather than just respond, we can foster open and honest communication with others. Lastly, emotional intelligence plays a significant role in managing interpersonal relationships.

By being mindful of our own emotions and practicing empathy and effective communication, we can build healthier and more fulfilling connections with others. This involves recognizing and respecting boundaries, resolving conflicts peacefully, and nurturing a supportive and positive environment for everyone involved. In conclusion, emotional intelligence is an essential skill set for nurturing our emotional well-being and fostering personal growth.

By cultivating self-awareness, developing emotional regulation, practicing empathy, refining communication skills, and nurturing healthy relationships, we can navigate through life with greater resilience, authenticity, and satisfaction. Let us embrace emotional intelligence as a lifelong journey of self-discovery and empowerment and create a world where emotional well-being is prioritized and cherished.

Chapter 6

Cultivating Mindfulness: Finding Balance in a Chaotic World

In today's fast-paced and chaotic world, finding balance and inner peace can feel like an elusive goal. We are constantly bombarded with distractions and demands, making it difficult to stay present and connected to ourselves and the world around us. However, by cultivating mindfulness, we can learn to navigate this chaos and find a sense of tranquility and harmony in our lives.

Mindfulness is the practice of being fully present at the moment, without judgment or attachment to the past or future. It involves paying attention to our thoughts, emotions, and physical sensations with curiosity and acceptance. By bringing our awareness to the present moment, we can detach from the worries and stressors that often consume us and instead focus on what is happening right now.

One way to cultivate mindfulness is through meditation. Taking just a few minutes each day to sit in stillness and observe our breath can have profound effects on our well-being. Through meditation, we learn to quiet the mind and develop a greater sense of clarity and calm. It allows us to detach from the constant stream of thoughts and worries that often plague us, and instead become fully present in the here and now.

Another practice that can help cultivate mindfulness is bringing awareness to our daily activities. Whether it's eating, walking, or even brushing our teeth, we can choose to engage fully in these simple tasks, paying attention to the sensations, tastes, and sounds that accompany them. By doing so, we bring a sense of intentionality and presence to our daily routines, transforming them from mundane chores to opportunities for mindfulness.

Additionally, practicing gratitude can also enhance our mindfulness and overall well-being. By regularly acknowledging and appreciating the positive aspects of our lives, we shift our focus from what is lacking to what is abundant. This cultivates a sense of contentment and gratitude, allowing us to experience greater joy and fulfillment in our daily lives.

Furthermore, incorporating mindfulness into our interactions with others can greatly improve our relationships. By being fully present and attentive when we engage in conversation, we show others that they are valued and respected. We can also become more attuned to their needs and emotions, fostering deeper connections and empathy.

In conclusion, cultivating mindfulness is a powerful tool for finding balance and peace in the midst of life's chaos. By practicing meditation, bringing awareness to our daily activities, expressing gratitude, and engaging mindfully in our interactions with others, we can reclaim our sense of presence, find inner calm, and navigate through life with greater clarity and authenticity.

Let us embrace mindfulness as a way of life and welcome the profound benefits it offers us in our pursuit of well-being and fulfillment.

CHAPTER 7

LETTING GO: RELEASING ATTACHMENTS AND MOVING FORWARD

In our journey toward personal growth and self-discovery, one of the most important lessons we must learn is the art of letting go. We often hold onto things, people, and situations that no longer serve us, causing unnecessary stress and preventing us from moving forward in our lives.

By releasing attachments and embracing the process of letting go, we create space for new possibilities and experiences to enter our lives.

Attachment can manifest in many forms - it could be a material possession, a relationship, a job, or even a belief or identity we cling to. It is often driven by fear and a sense of scarcity as if letting go means losing something valuable or stable.

However, the truth is that holding on too tightly can suffocate our growth and limit our potential.

Letting go does not mean dismissing the significance of what we are releasing, but rather acknowledging its place in our past and allowing ourselves to move forward.

It involves accepting that change is inevitable and

necessary for personal evolution. By releasing attachments, we create space for new opportunities, relationships, and possibilities to enter our lives.

One powerful practice to facilitate the process of letting go is forgiveness. Holding onto grudges and resentments only weighs us down and prevents us from experiencing true peace and freedom.

Forgiveness does not mean condoning or forgetting the actions of others, but rather freeing ourselves from the negative emotions and baggage associated with the situation. It is a gift we give ourselves, allowing us to release the past and move forward with compassion and understanding.

Another important aspect of letting go is cultivating self-compassion. Often, we hold onto self-judgment and past mistakes, which can hinder our growth and well-being. By practicing self-compassion, we learn to accept our imperfections and embrace our humanity. We recognize that we are all on a journey of growth and that making mistakes is a natural part of that process. By letting go of the need for perfection, we create space for self-growth and self-love.

Additionally, letting go may also involve setting boundaries in our relationships. Sometimes, we hold onto toxic or unfulfilling connections out of fear or obligation. However, by honoring our own needs and well-being, we can choose to let go of relationships that no longer align with our values and aspirations. This allows for more authentic and nourishing connections to come into our lives.

In conclusion, letting go is an essential part of our personal growth and transformation. By releasing attachments, practicing forgiveness, cultivating self-compassion, and setting healthy boundaries, we create space for new experiences and opportunities to unfold. Letting go is not always easy, but it is necessary for our well-being and happiness. So, let us have the courage to loosen our grip on what no longer serves us and embrace the freedom and growth that comes with letting go.

Chapter 8

Resilience: Bouncing Back from Adversity

Life is full of ups and downs, and we often face unforeseen challenges and setbacks along our journey. However, it is not the adversity itself that defines us; it is how we respond to it. In this chapter, we will explore the concept of resilience - the ability to bounce back from adversity and emerge stronger and wiser.

Resilience is not a trait that some people are born with and others lack; it is a skill that can be developed and cultivated. It involves our capacity to adapt, learn, and grow in the face of adversity. Resilience empowers us to navigate difficult situations with grace and fortitude, allowing us to overcome obstacles and achieve our goals.

One key aspect of building resilience is developing a positive mindset. Our thoughts and beliefs shape our reality, and by adopting a positive outlook, we can approach challenges with optimism and determination. This does not mean denying or minimizing the difficulties we face but rather choosing to focus on solutions, possibilities, and personal growth. Cultivating gratitude and practicing mindfulness can also contribute to a more resilient mindset.

Another important element of resilience is building a support network. Surrounding ourselves with trusted friends, family, or mentors can provide valuable emotional support and guidance during challenging times. Sharing our experiences and seeking assistance when needed can help alleviate the burdens we carry and remind us that we are not alone.

Additionally, resilience requires self-care. Taking care of our physical, mental, and emotional well-being is crucial in maintaining resilience and bouncing back from adversity. Engaging in activities that bring us joy and relaxation, practicing self-compassion, and prioritizing healthy habits contribute to our overall resilience and enable us to cope with stress more effectively.

Lastly, developing problem-solving skills and embracing a growth mindset are integral components of resilience. Rather than seeing obstacles as insurmountable roadblocks, resilient individuals view them as opportunities for learning and personal development. They approach challenges with curiosity, flexibility, and a willingness to adapt their strategies.

In conclusion, resilience is an essential skill that allows us to bounce back from adversity and grow stronger in the process. By cultivating a positive mindset, building a support network, practicing self-care, and embracing a growth mindset, we can enhance our resilience and face life's challenges with courage and determination. Remember, setbacks do not define us - it is our resilience that shapes our journey toward success and fulfillment.

Chapter 9

Strengthening
Relationships:
The Power of Connection

Human beings are inherently social creatures, and our relationships play a significant role in our overall well-being and happiness. Whether it is with family members, friends, romantic partners, or colleagues, the quality of our connections has a profound impact on our lives. In this chapter, we will explore the importance of strengthening relationships and the power of connection.

Building and maintaining healthy relationships requires effort, time, and open communication. It is essential to cultivate mutual respect, trust, and understanding in order to create a strong foundation. By nurturing our connections, we not only enrich our own lives but also contribute to the well-being of those around us.

One key aspect of strengthening relationships is active listening. When we truly listen to others, without judgment or interruption, we show them that we value their thoughts and feelings. This fosters a deeper sense of connection and allows for more meaningful and fulfilling interactions.

Another crucial element in building strong relationships is empathy. Empathy is the ability to understand and share the emotions of another person. By putting ourselves in someone else's shoes, we can better comprehend their experiences and perspectives. This helps us respond with compassion and support, deepening our connection with them.

In addition to active listening and empathy, expressing gratitude and appreciation towards our loved ones can have a transformative effect on our relationships. Showing genuine gratitude for the things they do, big or small, helps strengthen the bond we share. Simple acts of kindness and acknowledgment go a long way in fostering a positive and loving connection.

Furthermore, it is essential to resolve conflicts and disagreements in a healthy manner. Conflict is a natural part of any relationship, but how we handle it determines its impact. Approaching conflicts with an open mind, a willingness to compromise, and a focus on finding solutions rather than assigning blame promotes growth and harmony within our relationships.

Lastly, making time for meaningful connections is crucial. In our busy lives, it is easy to become consumed by tasks and responsibilities, neglecting the vital connections we have with others. By prioritizing quality time together, whether through shared activities, meaningful conversations, or simply being present with one another, we nourish our relationships and create lasting memories.

In conclusion, strengthening relationships is a fundamental aspect of living a fulfilling and happy life.

Through active listening, empathy, gratitude, conflict resolution, and prioritizing quality time, we can deepen our connections and experience the power of genuine human connection. Remember, strong relationships are built on love, trust, and a willingness to invest in the growth and well-being of those we care about.

CHAPTER 10

BUILDING BOUNDARIES: HONORING YOUR NEEDS AND PRIORITIES

In our journey towards self-growth and well-being, it is vital to establish and maintain healthy boundaries. Boundaries act as a protective shield, safeguarding our physical, emotional, and mental well-being. They allow us to set limits on what we are comfortable with and protect ourselves from being taken advantage of or overwhelmed.

Building boundaries begins with self-awareness. Understanding our needs, values, and priorities is essential in determining the boundaries we want to set. By taking the time to reflect on what truly matters to us, we can identify where we need to establish boundaries and communicate them effectively to others.

A crucial aspect of setting boundaries is learning to say no. Many of us struggle with saying no because we fear disappointing others or being seen as selfish. However, saying no is an act of self-care and self-respect. It allows us to honor our needs and prioritize our well-being.

Communication plays a significant role in setting and maintaining boundaries. Clearly and assertively expressing our boundaries helps others understand our limits and expectations. It is crucial to be respectful but firm in our communication, ensuring that our boundaries are upheld and valued.

Sometimes, people may push against our boundaries or disregard them entirely. In such situations, it is essential to stand firm, reassert our boundaries, and enforce consequences if necessary. Remember, it is not our responsibility to accommodate others at the expense of our own well-being.

Building boundaries also involves recognizing and respecting the boundaries of others. Just as we have the right to set our own limits, we must understand and honor the boundaries of those around us. This fosters mutual respect, trust, and healthier relationships overall.

Furthermore, self-care is an integral part of building boundaries. Taking care of our physical, emotional, and mental needs helps us maintain healthy boundaries. Engaging in activities that bring us joy, practicing self-care rituals, and prioritizing rest and relaxation all contribute to our overall well-being and reinforce the importance of boundaries.

In conclusion, building boundaries is a crucial aspect of self-growth and well-being. By establishing and maintaining healthy boundaries, we honor our needs and priorities, protect our well-being, and foster healthier relationships. Remember, setting boundaries is not selfish; it is an act of self-respect and self-care. Embrace the power of boundaries and experience the freedom and empowerment that comes with honoring your needs.

Chapter 11

Setting Goals and Taking Action: The Path to Accomplishment

In our journey toward personal and professional growth, setting goals and taking action are essential steps toward accomplishing our dreams and aspirations. Goals provide us with a roadmap, guiding us toward success and fulfillment. They allow us to focus our energy and efforts in a purposeful manner.

Setting goals begins with clarity of vision. We must have a clear understanding of what we want to achieve and why it is important to us. By defining our goals and aligning them with our values and passions, we create a sense of purpose that fuels our motivation and determination.

Once we have clarified our goals, it is crucial to break them down into smaller, manageable tasks. This helps us create a step-by-step plan of action, making our goals more attainable and less overwhelming. Each task completed brings us one step closer to our ultimate goal, boosting our confidence and momentum along the way.

To ensure our goals remain achievable and realistic, it is important to set specific, measurable, attainable, relevant, and time-bound (SMART) objectives. By having clear markers of progress and deadlines, we hold ourselves accountable and stay focused on our goals.

Taking action is the key to turning our goals into reality. It requires commitment, discipline, and perseverance. It is normal to encounter obstacles and setbacks along the way, but it is how we respond to these challenges that determine our success. Embracing a positive mindset and viewing setbacks as opportunities for growth and learning can help us stay resilient and motivated.

Furthermore, seeking support from others can greatly enhance our chances of success. Surrounding ourselves with a network of like-minded individuals, mentors, or coaches can provide guidance, encouragement, and accountability. Their insights and experiences can offer valuable perspectives and help us navigate through challenges more effectively.

Celebrating small victories and milestones is crucial in maintaining motivation and momentum. Acknowledging our progress and giving ourselves permission to celebrate each step forward reinforces our determination and inspires us to keep pushing toward our goals. In conclusion, setting goals and taking action are integral components of achieving our dreams and aspirations.

By clarifying our vision, breaking down our goals, staying accountable, and embracing a positive mindset, we can overcome obstacles and turn our dreams into reality. Remember, you have the power to create the life you desire. Begin today, set your goals, take action, and embark on the path to accomplishment.

CHAPTER 12

FACING FEAR:
EMBRACING COURAGE AND
STEPPING INTO THE UNKNOWN

Fear, although often seen as a negative emotion, is an inherent part of the human experience. It can hold us back from reaching our full potential and prevent us from pursuing our dreams. However, by learning to face our fears and embracing courage, we can break free from the limitations they impose and step into the unknown with confidence.

Fear can manifest in various forms, such as fear of failure, fear of rejection, or fear of the unknown. It stems from our instinctual desire for safety and security, but it can also paralyze us and hinder our growth. Recognizing our fears and understanding their underlying causes is the first step toward overcoming them.

To confront our fears, we must cultivate courage. Courage is not the absence of fear but rather the willingness to act in spite of it. It is a quality that can be developed and strengthened over time through practice and mindset shifts.

One effective strategy for facing fear is gradual exposure. By gradually exposing ourselves to situations that make us uncomfortable, we can desensitize our fear response and build resilience. This approach allows us to take small steps towards conquering our fears, rather than overwhelming ourselves with giant leaps.

Another powerful tool in overcoming fear is reframing our mindset. Instead of viewing fear as a barrier, we can choose to see it as an opportunity for growth. By shifting our perspective and embracing challenges as catalysts for personal development, we can transform fear into motivation.

Self-compassion is also crucial when facing fear. It is important to acknowledge and accept our fears without judgment or self-criticism. Recognizing that fear is a natural part of the human experience allows us to be kinder to ourselves and gives us the strength to move forward.

Stepping into the unknown requires a leap of faith. It means letting go of our attachment to certainty and embracing the possibilities that lie beyond our comfort zone. It is in the unknown where we discover new experiences, learn and grow, and find fulfillment.

When we face our fears and step into the unknown, we open ourselves up to a world of opportunities and personal transformation. We become more resilient, adaptable, and confident. Each act of courage becomes a stepping stone toward a life filled with purpose and fulfillment.

In conclusion, fear is a natural part of our journey, but it doesn't have to define our lives. By facing our fears, cultivating courage, and stepping into the unknown, we unlock our true potential and create a life of significance. Remember, you have within you the power to conquer your fears and embrace the endless possibilities that await you.

CHAPTER 13

SELF-COMPASSION: EMBRACING IMPERFECTIONS AND PRACTICING SELF-CARE

In a world that often emphasizes perfection and achievement, self-compassion is a powerful tool for nurturing our well-being and embracing our imperfections. It involves treating ourselves with kindness, understanding, and acceptance, just as we would treat a dear friend.

Self-compassion starts with recognizing our inherent worthiness and acknowledging that we are deserving of love, care, and compassion - both from others and from ourselves. It means letting go of self-judgment and unrealistic expectations, and instead, offering ourselves unconditional support and understanding.

Practicing self-compassion involves several key elements. First and foremost, it requires self-kindness. This means being gentle and understanding towards ourselves when we make mistakes or face challenges. Instead of berating ourselves with negative self-talk, we offer words of encouragement and support.

Another important aspect of self-compassion is recognizing our shared humanity. We all experience pain, struggle, and imperfections. Understanding that we are not alone in our challenges can help cultivate a sense of connection and empathy towards ourselves and others.

Self-compassion also entails mindfulness. By being present at the moment and observing our thoughts and feelings without judgment, we can develop a greater awareness of our needs and respond to them with kindness. Mindfulness allows us to navigate difficult emotions and experiences with grace and acceptance.

A crucial part of self-compassion is practicing self-care. This involves prioritizing our physical, emotional, and mental well-being. It means listening to our bodies, engaging in activities that bring us joy and relaxation, and setting healthy boundaries. Self-care is not selfish; it is an act of self-love and an investment in our overall happiness and fulfillment.

When we embrace self-compassion, we free ourselves from the burdens of perfectionism, self-criticism, and comparison. We learn to accept our flaws and imperfections as part of our unique journey. Rather than seeking external validation, we find solace and strength within ourselves.

Self-compassion is not always easy, especially if we have spent years internalizing self-judgment and criticism. However, with practice and patience, we can cultivate a kind and supportive relationship with ourselves. Each small act of self-compassion adds up and creates a positive ripple effect in our lives.

In conclusion, self-compassion is a transformative

practice that allows us to embrace our imperfections, prioritize our well-being, and nurture a compassionate relationship with ourselves. By treating ourselves with kindness and practicing self-care, we can create a foundation of resilience, self-worth, and inner strength. Remember, you deserve compassion and care, just as much as anyone else.

CHAPTER 14

SEEKING SUPPORT: THE IMPORTANCE OF COMMUNITY AND MENTORSHIP

In our journey towards personal growth and development, seeking support from others is crucial. Building a strong community and finding mentors can provide us with guidance, inspiration, and a sense of belonging. Surrounding ourselves with like-minded individuals who share our goals and values can greatly enhance our overall well-being and help us reach our full potential.

Community plays a vital role in our lives. It offers an environment where we can connect with others who understand and support us on our journey. Whether it's through friends, family, or interest-based groups, being part of a community helps us feel connected, valued, and accepted.

Communities provide a safe space to learn, grow, and exchange ideas. They offer encouragement and celebrate our successes, while also providing a support system during challenging times. Through shared experiences and perspectives, communities foster personal and collective growth.

Within our communities, mentors play a significant role. A mentor is someone who has walked a similar path, possesses knowledge and experience in a specific area, and is willing to guide and support us along our own journey. They act as a source of wisdom, motivation, and encouragement.

Having a mentor can offer numerous benefits. They can provide guidance and advice from their own experiences, helping us navigate challenges and make informed decisions. Mentors can also offer valuable networking opportunities and introduce us to new resources and perspectives.

Finding a suitable mentor involves identifying individuals who align with our goals and values. It's important to seek someone who is willing to invest their time and energy into our growth and development. Building a mentor-mentee relationship requires open communication, trust, and a mutual commitment to learning and growth.

To seek support from our community and mentors, we must be willing to ask for help and be open to receiving it. It's not a sign of weakness but rather a strength to recognize that we cannot navigate our journey alone. By reaching out and being vulnerable, we allow others to contribute to our growth and offer their support.

In addition to seeking support, we also have the opportunity to become mentors ourselves. By sharing our knowledge, experiences, and insights, we can inspire and guide others on their own journeys. Becoming a mentor not only helps others but also reinforces our own learning and growth.

In conclusion, seeking support from our community and mentors is vital for personal growth. Surrounding ourselves with like-minded individuals who share our goals, values, and interests creates a supportive environment where we can thrive.

Finding mentors who can provide guidance and wisdom helps us navigate our journey with greater clarity and confidence. Remember, you are never alone on your path to personal development - reach out and embrace the power of community and mentorship.

CHAPTER 15

EMBRACING VULNERABILITY:
OPENING TO AUTHENTIC
CONNECTIONS

In a world that often encourages us to put up walls and portray a perfect image, embracing vulnerability is a powerful way to foster authentic connections with others. By allowing ourselves to be seen and heard as our true selves, we create the space for genuine relationships to flourish. Vulnerability is often misunderstood as weakness, but, it is an act of courage.

It takes strength to open ourselves up to the possibility of rejection or judgment. However, when we embrace vulnerability, we invite others to do the same, creating an environment of trust, empathy, and understanding.

When we show vulnerability, we allow others to truly know us - our fears, hopes, dreams, and struggles.

This deepens the connection and builds a sense of intimacy that cannot be achieved through superficial interactions. Authentic connections are built on a foundation of honesty and vulnerability. To embrace vulnerability, it's essential to cultivate self-acceptance and self-compassion. Understanding and accepting ourselves, flaws, and all, allows us to share our true selves with others without fear of judgment. When we learn to be kind to ourselves, we can show up authentically in our relationships.

Opening to vulnerability requires creating a safe space with those around us. Surrounding ourselves with people who respect and honor our vulnerabilities encourages us to let our guard down and be our authentic selves. These connections become a source of support and validation, as we find comfort in knowing we are accepted for who we truly are.

However, it's important to note that not everyone will respond positively to our vulnerability, and that's okay. We cannot control how others react, but we can choose to surround ourselves with individuals who appreciate and value our openness. It's better to have a few meaningful connections than many shallow ones.

Embracing vulnerability also means being willing to listen and hold space for others' vulnerabilities. By empathetically listening and offering support, we create a reciprocal dynamic that strengthens our relationships. When we open ourselves up to others, they are more likely to reciprocate, deepening the bond of trust and connection. Authentic connections flourish when we are honest about our feelings, needs, and desires. Clear communication allows for understanding and creates a foundation for building deeper connections. It's essential to express ourselves openly and respectfully, fostering an environment where vulnerability is welcomed and celebrated.

In conclusion, embracing vulnerability is vital for

developing authentic connections with others. When we allow ourselves to be vulnerable, we create a space for genuine relationships to thrive. By accepting and embracing our own vulnerabilities, we pave the way for deeper connections founded on trust and empathy. Remember, it's in our moments of vulnerability that true connection and growth can occur. Open up, be brave, and embrace the power of authentic connections.

CHAPTER 16

ENHANCING WELL-BEING: NOURISHING THE BODY, MIND, AND SOUL

Taking care of our well-being is essential for a fulfilling and balanced life. Nourishing our body, mind, and soul allows us to thrive and find greater happiness and contentment. In this chapter, we will explore various practices and habits that can enhance our overall well-being.

Nourishing our body involves adopting healthy habits such as eating nutritious foods, staying active, and getting enough rest. A well-balanced diet provides the necessary nutrients for our bodies to function optimally. Regular exercise not only keeps us physically fit but also boosts our mood and reduces stress.

Prioritizing sufficient sleep allows our bodies to rejuvenate and maintain optimal health.

In addition to physical well-being, nurturing our minds is crucial. Engaging in activities that challenge our cognitive abilities, such as reading, puzzles, or learning something

47

new, helps keep our minds sharp and prevents cognitive decline.

Taking time for relaxation and stress management techniques, such as meditation or deep breathing exercises, promotes mental clarity and reduces anxiety.

Nourishing our souls involves connecting with our inner selves and finding meaning in our lives.

Engaging in activities that bring us joy and fulfillment, whether it be through creative outlets like art or music, spending time in nature, or practicing spirituality, are all ways to nourish our souls. Cultivating gratitude and practicing self-care are also important components of soul nourishment.

To enhance our overall well-being, it's essential to create a balanced and holistic approach. Finding a healthy equilibrium between our physical, mental, and spiritual needs is key. Making self-care a priority, setting boundaries, and seeking support from loved ones are all integral parts of nourishing our well-being.

Remember, enhancing well-being is a lifelong journey. It's important to regularly reassess and adjust our self-care routines based on our evolving needs. Embracing self-compassion and being gentle with ourselves during challenging times is crucial. Each step we take towards enhancing our well-being brings us closer to living a more joyful and fulfilling life.

In conclusion, nourishing our body, mind, and soul is the foundation for enhancing our overall well-being. By adopting healthy habits and engaging in activities that bring us joy and fulfillment, we create a harmonious balance in our lives. Remember to prioritize self-care, seek support when needed, and be kind to yourself along the way. May your journey towards enhanced well-being be filled with abundance and happiness.

Chapter 17

Harnessing the Power of Positive Thinking: Shifting Perspectives

Our thoughts have a tremendous impact on our overall well-being and outlook on life. The power of positive thinking lies in its ability to shift our perspectives, enabling us to see the world with more optimism and gratitude. In this chapter, we will explore the benefits of positive thinking and learn techniques to cultivate a positive mindset.

Positive thinking involves consciously choosing to focus on the positive aspects of life, even in the face of challenges or adversity. It is not about denying or ignoring the negative but rather acknowledging it without letting it consume our thoughts and emotions.

By retraining our minds to embrace a positive outlook, we can experience greater resilience, happiness, and overall well-being.

One technique for cultivating a positive mindset is practicing gratitude. Taking time each day to reflect on the things we are grateful for helps shift our attention from what's lacking to what's abundant in our lives. By appreciating the little joys and blessings, we can cultivate a sense of contentment and appreciation.

Another powerful tool for positive thinking is reframing. This involves consciously challenging negative thoughts and replacing them with more positive and empowering ones. By reframing our perceptions, we can transform obstacles into opportunities and setbacks into lessons for growth.

Surrounding ourselves with positivity is also crucial. Engaging in activities and spending time with people who uplift and inspire us can significantly impact our mindset. Seeking out motivational books, and podcasts, or joining supportive communities can provide a constant source of positivity and encouragement.

One important aspect of positive thinking is self-compassion. It's vital to be gentle and understanding with ourselves when we encounter setbacks or negative emotions. Embracing self-care practices, practicing mindfulness, and cultivating a non-judgmental attitude toward ourselves can foster a more positive and compassionate mindset.

In conclusion, harnessing the power of positive thinking is a transformative practice that can enhance our overall well-being. By consciously choosing to shift our perspectives and cultivate gratitude, reframe negative thoughts, surround ourselves with positivity, and practice self-compassion, we can experience greater joy, resilience, and contentment in our lives. Embrace the power of positive thinking and watch as it transforms your world.

Chapter 18

The Art of Forgiveness: Healing Wounds and Letting Go of Resentment

Forgiveness is a powerful practice that allows us to heal wounds, both within ourselves and in our relationships with others. Holding onto resentment and anger can weigh us down and hinder our personal growth. In this chapter, we will explore the art of forgiveness and discover how it can bring about healing and freedom.

Forgiveness is not about condoning or forgetting the harm that has been done to us. It is a choice to release ourselves from the pain and negative emotions associated with past hurts. By forgiving, we free ourselves from the burden of holding onto grudges and open the door to healing and transformation.

One of the first steps towards forgiveness is acknowledging our feelings and allowing ourselves to fully experience the pain. It is essential to give ourselves permission to grieve and process the emotions that arise. By doing so, we create space for healing and acceptance.

To truly forgive, it is important to cultivate empathy and understanding. Recognizing that everyone makes mistakes and has the capacity to grow allows us to see the humanity in others. By putting ourselves in their shoes, we can develop compassion and a willingness to let go of resentment.

Self-forgiveness is just as crucial as forgiving others. Often, we hold onto guilt and self-blame for past actions or decisions. However, by practicing self-compassion and understanding, we can release ourselves from the grip of self-judgment and embrace forgiveness.

It's important to note that forgiveness does not always mean reconciliation or maintaining a relationship with the person who has hurt us. Sometimes, it is necessary to set boundaries and prioritize our own well-being. Forgiveness is ultimately about finding inner peace and freeing ourselves from the emotions that hold us back.

In conclusion, the art of forgiveness is a transformative practice that allows us to heal wounds and let go of resentment. By acknowledging our feelings, cultivating empathy, practicing self-forgiveness, and setting boundaries, when necessary, we can experience profound healing and find a sense of freedom. Embrace the power of forgiveness and watch as it brings about positive changes in your life.

Chapter 19

Embracing Change:
Embodying Adaptability
and Flexibility

Change is an inevitable part of life. It can be both exciting and challenging, and our ability to adapt and be flexible in the face of change is essential for personal growth and well-being. In this chapter, we will explore the art of embracing change and learn how to embody adaptability and flexibility.

Embracing change starts with a mindset shift. Instead of resisting or fearing change, we can choose to view it as an opportunity for growth and development. By adopting a positive attitude towards change, we open ourselves up to new possibilities and experiences.

To embody adaptability, it is necessary to cultivate self-awareness. Understanding our own strengths and weaknesses allows us to identify areas where we may need to adapt and grow. Being open to feedback and willing to learn from our mistakes enables us to navigate change more effectively.

Flexibility involves being able to adjust our plans and expectations when circumstances change. It requires letting go of rigid thinking and being open to new ideas. By developing a flexible mindset, we can better navigate the twists and turns that life throws our way.

In times of change, it is important to practice self-care and prioritize our well-being. Taking care of our physical, emotional, and mental health equips us to handle the challenges that come with change. Self-care also helps us stay grounded and maintain resilience.

Building a support network is crucial for navigating change. Surrounding ourselves with positive, encouraging, and understanding individuals can provide us with a sense of community and offer support during times of uncertainty. Seeking guidance and advice from trusted mentors or friends can also help us gain perspective and find creative solutions.

In conclusion, embracing change requires embodying adaptability and flexibility. By adopting a positive mindset, cultivating self-awareness, practicing flexibility, prioritizing self-care, and building a support network, we can navigate change with grace and resilience.

Remember, change is an opportunity for growth and personal development. Embrace it, and watch as it brings about positive transformations in your life.

ABOUT THE AUTHOR

Raymond Penny is an empathetic and compassionate individual with a passion for assisting others on their journey toward personal growth and self-discovery. With a background in Business Management and a deep understanding of human nature, they have dedicated themselves to providing gentle guidance and support to those in need. Throughout their career, Raymond has worked in various roles, including counseling, coaching, and mentoring. They strongly believe in the power of empathy, active listening, and creating a safe space for individuals to explore their thoughts, emotions, and aspirations. Their writing reflects their genuine desire to help others navigate life's challenges with patience, understanding, and kindness. Whether through articles, stories, or helpful advice Raymond Penny strives to provide meaningful content that inspires personal growth and fosters positive connections. In addition to their professional pursuits, Raymond Penny enjoys spending time in nature, practicing mindfulness and meditation, and engaging in creative outlets such as writing, painting, or playing a musical instrument. These activities fuel their creativity and allow them to connect with their own inner voice, which they aim to share with others. Above all, Raymond Penny believes in the transformative power of human connection and the importance of cultivating a supportive and empathetic community. Through their work, they hope to uplift and empower individuals to embrace their true selves and live authentically. Raymond Penny welcomes you to reach out and connect, whether it be for guidance, collaboration, or simply to share stories and insights. They truly believe that we are all connected and that by supporting one another, we can create a kinder and more compassionate world.

ACKNOWLEDGMENTS

Writing a book is truly a labor of love, and it is impossible to bring such a project to fruition without the support and assistance of many individuals. I would like to take this opportunity to express my deepest gratitude to everyone who has contributed to the creation of "Unleashing the Power Within: The Journey to Personal Transformation." First and foremost, I would like to thank my adopted mom Jeanne Larrabee and Jean Colin for their unwavering love, encouragement, and belief in me. Their support has been an endless source of inspiration throughout this writing process.

I am also immensely grateful to best friends Tye J. Smith and Uncle Joshua Robert who provided invaluable feedback and insights. Your input helped shape the content of this book and make it more impactful. Thank you for your time, honesty, and willingness to share your perspectives. To my editor, thank you for your meticulous attention to detail and your dedication to bringing out the best in this manuscript. Your guidance and expertise have been instrumental in refining the ideas and ensuring that the message resonates with readers.

I would like to extend my appreciation to the team at the publishing house for their hard work, professionalism, and belief in this project. Your commitment to excellence is evident in every aspect of this book's production. A special thanks go out to all the mentors, coaches, and teachers who have influenced my personal growth and understanding of self-transformation. Your wisdom and guidance have had a profound impact on my life and have greatly enriched the content of this book. Lastly, I want to express my heartfelt gratitude to the readers. Without your support and interest, this book would not have a purpose.

It is my sincerest hope that "Unleashing the Power Within" helps you in your journey toward personal transformation and empowers you to create the life you dream of.

To all those who have played a part, big or small, in the creation of this book, please accept my deepest gratitude. Your contributions have been invaluable, and I am truly honored to have had the opportunity to work with you all. Thank you.

Raymond M Penny

Made in the USA
Columbia, SC
22 June 2024

37150055R00039